This book presented to

TO:

Mrs. Hazama

Love,

Austin &

Ashley

Tesoriero

BPP-35890   Design by Evelia Sowash   © 2003 Antioch Publishing

JOHN MUIR

America's Naturalist

BY THOMAS LOCKER

Fulcrum Publishing
Golden, Colorado

Library of Congress Cataloging-in-Publication Data

Locker, Thomas, 1937–
John Muir, America's naturalist / by Thomas Locker.
p. cm.
Summary: Presents an overview of the life of the naturalist who founded
the Sierra Club and was influential in establishing the national park system.
ISBN 1-55591-393-8 (hardcover : alk. paper)
1. Muir, John, 1838-1914—Juvenile literature. 2. Naturalists—United
States—Biography—Juvenile literature. 3. Conservationists—United
States—Biography—Juvenile literature. [1. Muir, John, 1838-1914.
2. Naturalists. 3. Conservationists.] I. Title.
QH31.M9L63 2003
508.794'092—dc21

2002153593

Design by Nancy Duncan-Cashman
Printed in China
0 9 8 7 6 5 4 3 2 1

Fulcrum Publishing
16100 Table Mountain Parkway, Suite 300
Golden, Colorado 80403
(800) 992-2908 • (303) 277-1623
www.fulcrum-books.com

Many books have been written about John Muir, but his life is still a fresh source of interest and inspiration to each generation. He sparked the preservationist movement in the United States—indeed throughout the whole world. He had a marvelous ability to connect the scenic with the spiritual world. His unique skill with words made the scenes of nature come alive before the eyes of the reader. This book brings John Muir to all readers, both the young and the young at heart. As a lifetime follower of his, I know that John would have liked that.

John Muir was a farseeing prophet who pointed out that in nature "everything in the world was connected to everything else." He meant the boulders, as well as the flowers, the animals, and all humankind. The lands and rivers and mountains are all included.

One hundred ten years ago, Muir was the leader in the founding of the Sierra Club, an organization that to this day carries on the work he began long ago of encouraging citizen action to protect the natural world. Equally at home in the wildernesses of California and of Alaska, Muir wrote charming lyrical descriptions of flowers, trees, and mountains for the benefit of future generations. I commend the beautiful and inspirational writings of John Muir to the readers of this book.

—*Dr. Edgar Wayburn*
Honorary President of the Sierra Club

*H*igh up in the Sierra Mountains of California

is a valley called Yosemite.

Every year millions of people come to

see "this special temple of Nature,

an immense hall flanked by granite cliffs

and thundering waterfalls."

"One learns that the world, though made, is yet being made. That this is still the morning of creation."

It was in Yosemite that a lean and grizzly bearded man named John Muir learned to see Nature in a new way. By sharing his love of the wild with others, he changed the way many people think about the natural world.

"The clouds come and go among the cliffs like living creatures."

John Muir was born in Scotland in 1838.

When John was eleven years old, his family sailed

across the Atlantic Ocean to the United States.

His father, a devout and strict man, decided to

start a farm in Wisconsin.

*"All that the
sun shines on is
beautiful, so long
as it is wild."*

While carving a homestead out of the wilderness, John listened to his father preach from the Bible. His father tried to convince John that Nature was God's gift to man to use as a resource. John worked very hard and grew up lean and strong willed, but he soon began to form his own ideas about Nature.

"Any fool can destroy trees. They cannot run away . . ."

As a young man, John Muir worked as an inventor, until he temporarily lost his eyesight in a factory accident. While recovering, he made a huge decision—to leave the factory and devote his life to the study of Nature. When his eyesight returned, he set off and walked one thousand miles, from Indiana to the Gulf of Mexico, making careful notes in his journal about the plants and animals he saw.

"Go to Nature's School—the one true university."

John's travels led him to California. He found a
job herding sheep in the high meadows near the
Yosemite Valley. When the sheep entered Yosemite,
John saw "the unforgettable skyline of sculptured
domes and spires." The beauty took his breath
away.

*"The clearest way
to the universe is
through a forest
wilderness."*

Yosemite had a powerful effect on John Muir. He moved to the valley and for years took odd jobs, which left him plenty of time to hike and explore. He went up into the mountains in search of glaciers and into the groves of gigantic and ancient trees. Yosemite became his home.

"People are beginning to find out that going to the mountains is going home, that wilderness is a necessity."

In the groves of ancient trees, John studied the ways of the animals: the bears, deer, squirrels, and even the tiny ants. He called the soaring trees the "tree people." He identified the different kinds of pines and fir trees and made drawings of the noble redwoods and the ancient Sequoia. Some of the Sequoia were thousands of years old.

"Everything is hitched to everything else in the universe."

When furious storms swept through Yosemite,
John Muir was delighted. He loved the wildness
of Nature. To get even closer to the howling winds
of the storm, he climbed to the top of a bucking
Douglas fir and hung on, swaying and listening.

"The winds blow their
own freshness into
you, and the storms
their energy, while
cares will drop off like
autumn leaves."

John Muir stayed in Yosemite year-round. He loved winter and was known to disappear into the mountains for days. He treaded lightly, without a blanket, carrying only some bread and tea. One day, after climbing up a long snow-covered slope, he heard an avalanche beginning. John sat down, lifted his feet, and slid on the crest safely to the floor of the valley.

"The winter clouds grow, and bloom, and shed their starry crystals on every leaf and rock."

When it came time for John to settle down,

he married and became the father of two girls.

John ran a farm in the valley, but continually

returned to his beloved Yosemite. He became

upset when lumber interests and cattlemen

began closing in. At the urging of his friends,

John started writing to encourage the preservation

of the wilderness.

*"Everybody needs
beauty as well as
bread . . ."*

John Muir became well known. People loved his writing. Powerful, rich, and important people— philosophers, scientists, industrialists, even the president of the United States—came to meet the rugged mountain man. John helped start the Sierra Club, one of the first organizations devoted to preserving wilderness.

"In God's wildness lies the hope of the world— the great fresh unblighted, unredeemed wilderness."

A tireless political crusader in the fight to create National Parks, John Muir talked with the legislators in California and Washington, D.C. He wrote books and articles. John won many battles and lost some. Still, he found time to explore the glaciers of Alaska and other wilderness areas all over the world.

"Wildness . . . bestows a new sense of Earth's beauty and size."

John Muir's years of wandering in the wilderness led him to a deeper way of seeing Nature. Everything from the smallest snowflake to the farthest star were part of Nature, and man was not its master. Because of John Muir's gifts, people today can see Nature with new eyes.

"We all travel the Milky Way together, trees and men."

John Muir wrote extensively about Nature. Here are a few selections of his words.

"When I was a boy in Scotland, I was fond of everything that was wild, and all my life I've grown fonder and fonder of wild places and wild creatures."

"The grand show is eternal. It is always sunrise somewhere; the dew is never dried up at once; a shower is always falling; vapor ever rising. Eternal sunrise, eternal sunset, eternal dawn and gloaming, on sea and continents and islands, each in its turn, as the round earth rolls."

"Nature, like an enthusiastic gardener, could not resist the temptation to plant flowers everywhere."

"Climb the mountains and get good tidings. Nature's peace will flow into you as sunshine flows into the trees. The winds will blow their own freshness into you and the storms their energy, while care will drop off like autumn leaves."

"When we are with Nature, we are awake, and we discover many interesting things and reach many a mark we are not aiming at."

"It (Yosemite) is by far the grandest of all the special temples of Nature that I was ever permitted to enter."

"Only by going alone in silence, without baggage, can one truly get into the heart of the wilderness. All other travel is mere dust and hotels and baggage and chatter."

"A thousand Yellowstone wonders are calling. Look up and down and round about you."

"As age comes on, one source of enjoyment after another is closed, but Nature's sources never fail. Like a generous host, she offers her brimming cup in endless variety, served in a grand hall, the sky its ceiling, the mountains its walls, decorated with glorious paintings and enlivened with bands of music ever playing."

"There is a love of wild Nature in everybody, an ancient mother love ever showing itself whether recognized or no, and however covered by cares and duties."

"These temple destroyers, devotees of ravaging commercialism, seem to have a perfect contempt for Nature, and instead of lifting their eyes to God of the mountains, lift them to the Almighty Dollar."

"And surely all God's people, however serious or savage, great or small, like to play. Whales and elephants, dancing humming gnats, and invisibly small mischievous microbes— all are warm with divine radiance and must have lots of fun in them."

"Wander here a whole summer if you can. Thousands of God's blessings will search you and soak you as if you were a sponge and the big days will go by uncounted."

"The mountains are fountains of men as well as of rivers, of glaciers, of fertile soil. The great poets, philosophers, prophets, able men, whose thoughts and deeds have moved the world, have come down from the mountains."

"I only went out for a walk and finally concluded to stay out till sundown, for going out, I found, was really going in."